Drugs

What's That Got To Do With Me?

Drugs

Antony Lishak

FRANKLIN WATTS
LONDON • SYDNEY

First published in 2006 by
Franklin Watts
338 Euston Road
London
NW1 3BH

Franklin Watts Australia
Hachette Children's Books
Level 17/207 Kent Street
Sydney NSW 2000

Series editor: Adrian Cole
Design: Thomas Keenes
Art director: Jonathan Hair
Picture researcher: Sarah Smithies

A CIP catalogue record for this book is
available from the British Library.

ISBN: 0 7496 6394 4

Dewey Classification: 362.29

Printed in China

Acknowledgements:
Carrie Boretz/Corbis:22. Richard Gardner/REX Features: 6 (l),
20. David Hoffman Photo Library/Alamy: 17. Peter
Hosking/REX Features: Cover, 24. ImageState/Alamy: 4–5,
25, 28 (cl), (fr). LWA- JDC/Corbis: 6 (r), 12. Dennis Nett
/Syracuse Newspapers/The Image Works/Topfoto: 18. James
D. Morgan/REX Features: 14. Lehtikuva Oy/REX Features: 8,
32. Mark Peterson/Corbis: 13, 30. Photosport
International/REX Features: 26. John Powell/REX Features: 2,
19, 31. John Powell/Topfoto: Cover, 23, 28 (fl), (cr).
Photofusion Picture Library/Alamy: 11, 21, 29. Shout/Alamy:
9. Shout/REX Features: 7. Sipa Press/Rex Features: 6 (c), 16.
Bildagentur Franz Waldhaeusl/Alamy: 10. Max
Whittakker/Empics: 27, 28 (l), (r).

Contents

So what?

Drugs are everywhere in our world, in pharmacies, newsagents, off-licences and on street corners. Some of them are legal, like the painkillers people take for a headache. Others, like heroin, are illegal. There are people whose lives depend on both these types of drug.

What's it all about?

A drug is a substance that affects how our minds and bodies work. Drugs can be swallowed, inhaled or injected. People take legal or illegal drugs for lots of reasons: to relieve pain; to have fun; to win races; because they are addictive. In this book you will meet a selection of people whose lives have been affected by illegal drugs – a farmer whose crops are made into heroin, and a child with a drug-dealing father. You will also hear from people affected by legal drugs, from a child whose mum uses prescription drugs to a girl with a binge-drinking sister.

Personal accounts

All of the testimonies are true. Some are first-hand accounts, while others are the result of bringing similar experiences together to create a single "voice". Every effort has been made to ensure they are authentic. To protect identities, a few names have been changed and models have posed for some of the pictures. Wherever possible, permission to use the information has been obtained.

Ask yourself

The testimonies won't tell you all there is to know about drugs; that wouldn't be possible. Instead, as you encounter the different views, think about your own opinions and experiences. This will help you begin to address the question: "Drugs – what's that got to do with me?"

Drinking in a playground. Many legal drugs, such as alcohol, can be abused.

A drug addicted parent

Maria is 19 and worried that she won't be allowed to keep her newborn baby. She is addicted to an illegal drug called crack cocaine. Her baby was born addicted to the drug.

I don't want to lose my baby. The Social Services might say I'm not fit to look after her because I'm a junkie. Well that's not really fair. As soon as I found out I was pregnant I started to cut back and a special Maternity Drugs unit helped me.

Those first two days with my baby in the hospital were the best days of my life. I don't think I ever loved someone so much.

I couldn't touch her because she had lots of tubes in her. The doctor said that her body was dependent on the drugs I took when she was in my womb and now she is suffering withdrawal

Mother and baby. This baby may still be taken away from its mother.

Fact bank

■ Using crack cocaine during pregnancy reduces the flow of blood and food to the unborn child. These babies are often stillborn, or born very early.

■ In 2004 the Bristol Maternity Drugs Unit cared for over 100 pregnant drug addicts. 10% of those mothers were not allowed to keep their babies.

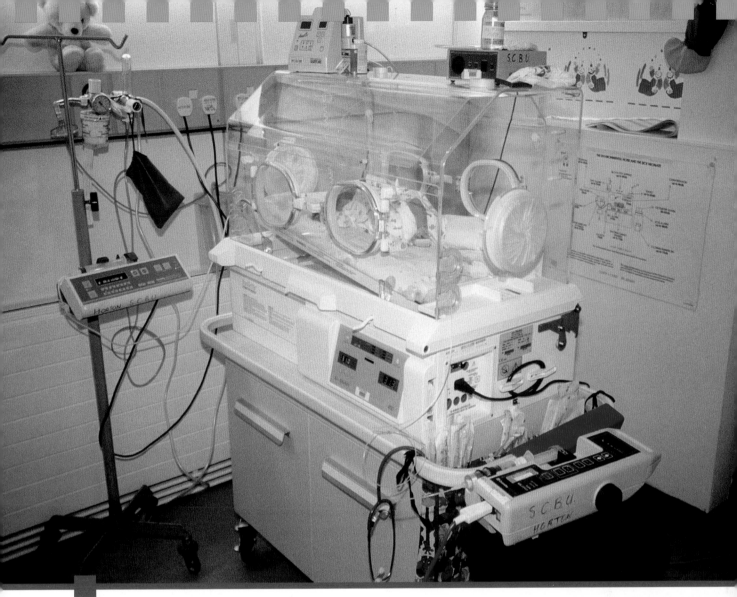

Baby in an incubator. Drug dependant babies are weak and need special care.

symptoms. That's why she hardly stops crying. I can't breast-feed her either, because the drug is in my milk.

They said it could be two months before she recovers and they don't know yet if there is any long-term damage to her brain. The nurses let me hold her this morning and said I was really good with her. But I know I'll have to be drug-free to keep her.

Ask yourself this...

■ Why didn't Maria stop taking drugs altogether during her pregnancy?

■ When, if ever, is it right to take a baby away from its mother?

■ What do you think will happen to Maria if her baby is taken away?

A pair of smokers

Joe is a life-long smoker who desperately wants to give up because of his failing health. Mike, his 15-year-old son, smokes as well, but has very different views.

Cigarettes are highly addictive.

Joe Rayner

I'm 50 – I've been a smoker since I was 14. Back in those days nobody knew it caused cancer or lung disease. My mum smoked more when she was pregnant with my sister "to keep the baby small"! I've tried everything to stop – acupuncture, hypnosis, gum, patches, but I think it's too late. My arteries are so thin now that I can hardly walk. I've already had one heart operation. The doctors say if I don't give up smoking in the next few months my legs will stop working and they'll have to be amputated. You'd have thought all this would have put my son off smoking.

Fact bank

■ Cigarettes contain nicotine, which is a highly addictive drug.

■ Smoking causes over 430,000 deaths in the US each year.

■ About 70% of current smokers would like to give up altogether.

■ In 2003, the UK government earned £8,093 million from tax on cigarettes.

Mike Rayner

Sometimes I run across the road without looking, so do millions of other people. It's dangerous, but I still do it. I also smoke. I know how harmful it is – just look at my dad. But he smokes twice as much as me, and only a few smokers are as unlucky as he's been. I don't like it when the "health police" kick me out of the youth club and make me stand in the street. What about the people using illegal drugs, they're breaking the law, but I'm not. And don't start complaining that hospitals spend too much time and money treating

Younger people who smoke find it harder to give up smoking in later life.

smokers with lung disease or whatever. I bet twice as much gets spent on people with addictions to heroin. Anyway, even if I did stop, I'd still be breathing in the smoke that fills the room when my dad lights up; it's called passive smoking. Just think about that next time someone near you is smoking – you're smoking too.

Ask yourself this...

■ How could Joe stop Mike smoking? What might he say to help persuade him to quit?

■ Do you think that Mike really doesn't want to stop or is he addicted to nicotine like his father?

A reluctant user

Michelle is 12 years old, and under pressure from her new friends. She had to compromise her beliefs to remain part of the crowd.

No one in my family smokes, but when I went to my new school all the people I hung out with did. I felt so left out. I was the only one who didn't smoke and it became such a big deal. So, in the end I gave in. I didn't really have a choice. Then one lunchtime, Cheryl took a joint out – she got it from her brother.

Young people are influenced strongly by their friends.

Fact bank

■ Cannabis is a type of illegal drug that can be smoked or eaten.

■ A "joint" is crushed cannabis leaves, rolled in cigarette paper and smoked. Cannabis makes the smoker feel relaxed and happy, but it can also induce anxiety and depression.

■ Some patients with serious medical conditions, such as cancer and multiple sclerosis, say cannabis use reduces pain and improves their quality of life.

■ Cannabis users under 18 are at more risk of developing mental health problems.

We were having a talk on drugs that afternoon, so she was just showing off. She lit it up and passed it around. Everyone knew it was wrong, but that's what made it exciting. It made us feel big – how could I refuse? I didn't even really inhale, I only had a tiny puff. In the talk, when our teacher asked if anyone had ever taken drugs, Cheryl was the only one who put her hand up. Afterwards she called the rest of us chickens, but I didn't care. At least I wasn't the only one.

These teenagers are taking part in a drugs awareness programme.

Ask yourself this...

■ Why do you think Cheryl was the only one to admit to taking drugs?

■ When have you been persuaded to do something you felt was wrong?

■ How much choice did Michelle have in this situation – and what choices is she going to have to make in the future?

■ If people underage can't buy cigarettes, where do they get them?

A drugs dog handler

Some dogs are specially trained to sniff out drugs with their sensitive noses. Here is one dog handler that has been called in by schools to help keep them drug-free.

This Australian police dog has been trained to detect a range of different drug smells.

This is Barney, and I'm his handler. Like all dogs his sense of smell is much stronger than humans. He has been trained to pick up the scent of drugs and is capable of finding cocaine, heroin, ecstasy and cannabis.

We usually work in pubs and clubs, but recently we have been called into schools.

Fact bank

■ A dog's sense of smell is almost 50 times more sensitive than a human's.

■ Dogs can be trained to pick out just one smell from a cocktail of different scents.

■ Dogs that work in schools are trained to just sit if they detect drugs, rather than attracting too much attention by barking loudly.

This dog has picked up a strong scent.

The aim is to prevent young people using drugs, rather than to find any. They might not take drugs if they know they are going to be caught.

First, I brought Barney in to demonstrate just how efficient he is at his job. I think that made quite an impression on the pupils – especially when he detected the smell of cannabis on a jacket that had been exposed to the drug two days earlier.

From what the headteacher says, the vast majority of parents are in favour of these tests. But then the majority of people don't take drugs. It's only those who have something to hide who would object. And if you did object then you would immediately look suspicious.

I think what I'm doing is making it easier for pupils to say no. I'm sure that most of them try the stuff, not because they want to, but because their friends do. If they can use me as an excuse not to take drugs, without losing face, then all well and good.

Ask yourself this...

■ Why are pupils checked for drugs if most of them are not drug users?

■ How could being checked for drugs affect your personal rights?

■ How do you think a visit from this drugs dog would have affected Michelle (see pages 12–13)?

A drugs farmer

Many drugs are made from plants. This farmer in Afghanistan makes his living growing opium poppies. The seeds are made into an addictive, illegal drug called heroin.

When you look at my fields you see opium poppies. Yes, they can be made into heroin. But to me poppies mean food and clothes for my family.

I used to grow wheat here. Before the end of 2001, when the Taliban were still in control, it was against the law to grow poppies. In those days breaking the law was too risky – my neighbour was in jail for over a year and his land was taken away. If his family hadn't lived with us they would have starved.

Our new government also says we mustn't grow this crop. But now we have democracy. I love democracy. To me it means when you break the law nothing happens to you! I have heard of a few fields being destroyed by aeroplanes that spray poison, but I have never seen it.

A farmer in Afghanistan in his opium poppy field.

Fact bank

■ Afghanistan is responsible for 75% of the world's heroin production.

■ Almost all of the world's cocaine comes from coca plants grown in Colombia, Peru and Bolivia.

■ Cannabis plants are grown across the globe.

■ Profits from the sale of illegal drugs are often used to fund criminal activity.

Harvesting opium poppies to be made into heroin.

Most of the families I know depend on this plant. I am very sorry to hear that people in other countries become ill on the drugs made from it, but I don't think it is my fault. If they didn't want their drugs then there wouldn't be such a big demand for my poppies.

I can earn ten times more than I would if I grew wheat. If you want to pay me the difference then I will cut my poppies down tomorrow.

Ask yourself this...

■ If you were this farmer, what would stop you growing poppies?

■ This farmer says that any bad effects caused by the drugs made from his crop are not his fault. Who would you blame?

■ Why do you think his government doesn't stop poppy production?

Son of a drug dealer

Here is a teenager who is surrounded by illegal drugs. Barry's dad supplies heroin to users. So far his dad has not been imprisoned, but what will happen to Barry when he is?

My dad used to take drugs, but he says it's a mug's game. Now he just sells them to other people on the estate. People used to call round to buy stuff, but the police started to hassle us. They arrested Dad for supplying, but he got off. Now people just phone him for drugs. He chooses a different place every day, so the police don't get suspicious. Sometimes I make deliveries for him on my bike. But I have to be careful – one of my mates got stopped and searched on his bike by the police the other day.

Visiting time at a prison. Drug dealers can receive long prison sentences.

I know drugs are wrong. But so many people need to take them. And they'll do anything to get the money – sell their own mum's wedding ring if they could! My dad says he's just "feeding the demand". And he bought me my new bike. He couldn't have done that before when he had no work.

A drug deal is carried out quickly on a street. Most drug dealers start life as drug users.

Fact bank

■ In the UK, people who are convicted of supplying heroin can be sentenced to life imprisonment.

■ In 2004, half the people detained by Australian police had used drugs.

■ Drug users in the USA are 16 times more likely to be arrested for theft than non-drug users.

Ask yourself this...

■ Who is more at fault here: the drug user who steals to feed a habit or the drug dealer who supplies the drugs? Why do you think that?

■ What do you think would happen to Barry if the next time his father is arrested he ends up with a prison sentence?

Prescription drugs

When we are ill doctors often write a prescription so that people can buy special drugs from a pharmacy. Here is the voice of someone whose life was improved after his mum started taking prescription drugs.

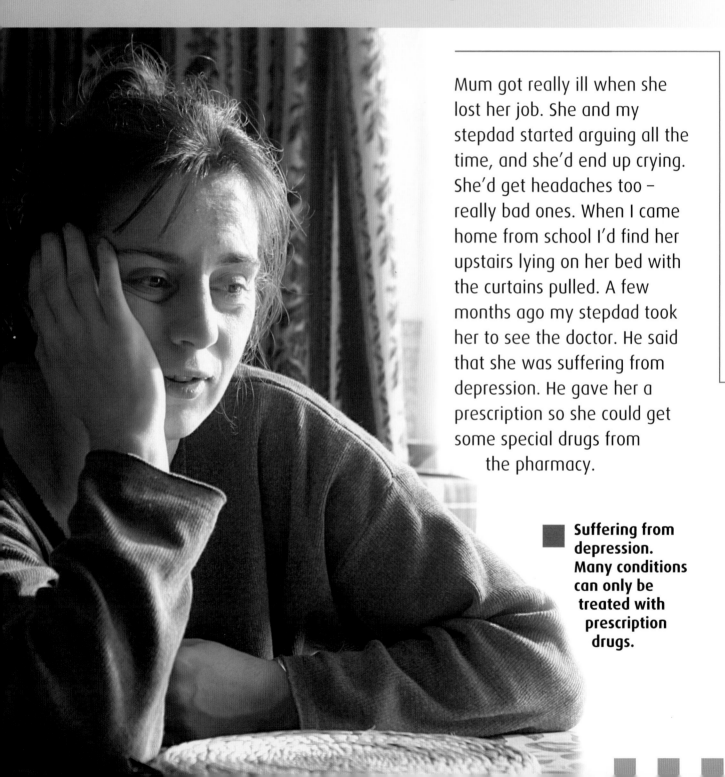

Mum got really ill when she lost her job. She and my stepdad started arguing all the time, and she'd end up crying. She'd get headaches too – really bad ones. When I came home from school I'd find her upstairs lying on her bed with the curtains pulled. A few months ago my stepdad took her to see the doctor. He said that she was suffering from depression. He gave her a prescription so she could get some special drugs from the pharmacy.

Suffering from depression. Many conditions can only be treated with prescription drugs.

Fact bank

■ Millions of people around the world are prescribed drugs every day.

■ Drugs prescribed to help someone suffering from depression are called "anti-depressants". Some doctors believe that counselling is very helpful too.

■ Approximately 4 million people in the USA abuse prescription drugs.

■ Some prescription drugs are addictive. Many people abuse them because they make them feel "high".

Counselling and prescription drugs can help to successfully tackle a range of illnesses.

It was like a miracle! Okay, it didn't happen straight away, but we've started to go to places again at the weekend. Everything is back the way it was. Except for mum's job of course. She sees a woman every week to talk about getting a new job. My stepdad said it's going to be really hard for all of us, but that we should take one step at a time. She has to take her drugs all the time now, she's not an addict though, she just needs them to be normal.

Ask yourself this...

■ When was the last time you were prescribed drugs by your doctor?

■ In what ways is this woman different from the young mother on pages 8–9?

■ What is the difference between using prescription drugs correctly, and abusing them?

Binge drinking

Cynthia has been binge drinking, and it's starting to affect her family in other ways. We hear from her younger sister – "the morning after the night before".

Cynthia came back from hospital this morning – she's been in her room ever since. Mum was with her all night, while Dad stayed at home to look after me. I could tell he was angry – all he said was "your silly sister drank herself unconscious".
I asked if she'll be okay and he replied "probably, but it'd serve her right if she wasn't". It was her 16th birthday. All her friends came round last night at about

Teenagers can find it difficult to deal with drink.

six o'clock to get ready to go out. They were meeting the rest of her mates at a club, I think. The last thing Dad said to her before they left was "go easy on the booze!".

This morning I heard Mum tell Dad not to be so hard on her, that she had learnt her lesson and he should be grateful that she was better. But he said that alcohol poisoning was serious and Cynthia should be made aware of

Fact bank

■ In the UK it is illegal to buy alcohol if you are under 18, and in many states in the USA you have to be over 21.

■ Drinking excessive amounts of alcohol leads to a loss of coordination, slowed reflexes, distorted vision and even blackouts.

■ Binge drinking is defined as consuming four or more alcoholic drinks in a row.

■ 65% of the youths surveyed in the US in 2004 said that they were given alcohol by family and friends.

Teenagers in a club. The success of a night out is often measured by how drunk people get.

how close she was to killing herself. Then Mum said he was being a hypocrite and reminded him of all the times he had phoned her to come and pick him up when he was too drunk to drive home. But Dad got really angry and said that was different. Then he shouted something like "I'm old enough to hold my drink. The fact I called you shows that I knew I was drunk!". I wonder if Cynthia heard him?

Ask yourself this...

■ At what age should a person be allowed to drink alcohol?

■ When, if ever, is it okay to get drunk?

■ If Cynthia did hear her dad, what might she have thought?

A gas user

Household substances, called solvents, give off toxic fumes that can be very dangerous, but they can also produce a "high". Here Alex explains what happened when he experimented with an everyday deodorant.

It started with my sister's deodorant. I went into the bathroom and it reeked of the stuff – but I thought it smelt nice.

Inhaling toxic fumes.

The can was on the shelf so I picked it up. I just wanted to see what a really strong blast of the stuff would smell like. So I sprayed it right up my nose and sniffed. It really made my head tingle. I'd never felt anything like it before. I felt a bit sick and it made my head spin.

Fact bank

■ Solvent abuse is the deliberate inhalation of fumes given off by some solvents. They are not illegal, but it is illegal for shops to sell them to young people.

■ Nearly a third of people who die from gas inhalation are first time users. They usually suffer a heart attack.

■ There is no safe way to inhale gas and other solvents.

The next thing I knew I was in hospital. I'd collapsed in the bathroom. The doctors say I was lucky that my mum found me when she did, because if she hadn't got me to the hospital in time I could have died. Now I've been grounded. Mum said she almost had a heart attack when she saw me lying on the floor.

Ask yourself this...

■ How much can you blame the boy, his mum, his sister and the manufacturer of the deodorant for this situation?

■ What could parents do to make children more aware of the dangers of inhaling solvents?

Recovering in hospital. Even a single blast of gas can prove fatal.

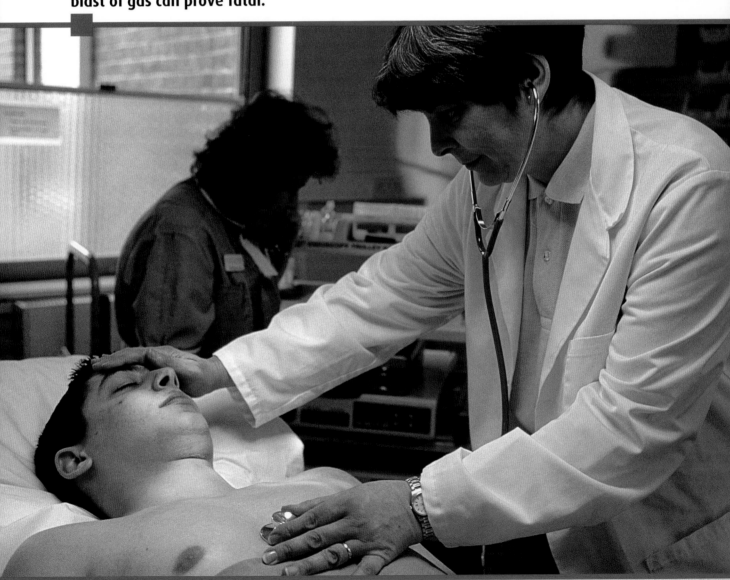

Drugs in sport

For some athletes the will to win takes over. Below we hear from banned British cyclist Dave Millar, and Craig Masback, director of the USA Track and Field team.

Dave Millar

I was one of the world's top cyclists. I had already won the World Championship by a huge margin. I didn't need to use drugs. But I got to a point where I wanted to win so much that I did something I didn't need to do. Then the drug police found two syringes in my flat. At first, I thought my lawyer

Fact bank

■ Some performance enhancing drugs aid muscle growth. Others reduce tiredness and enable athletes to train more intensively than normal.

■ Athletes are randomly tested for drugs during training and at events.

■ If an athlete is found to have cheated by taking an illegal enhancing drug they are usually banned. Some athletes are banned from the sport forever.

Dave Millar before he was banned.

could help me get away with it. But then I thought "What has my life come to – how can I live like this?" I could have kept fighting, but fundamentally I was living a lie and that's not good for anyone. I received a two-year ban from cycling and was stripped of my 2003 title. I know I made mistakes, but I am ready to learn and would like to explain the dangers of drugs to young riders.

Stopping the cheats

Many Track and Field teams have in the past been associated with stories of drugs cheats. But upcoming stars of the sport have been educated differently. Craig Masback, executive director of USA Track and Field team, supports a lifetime ban for drug cheats. "Certainly there is no athlete on the team that doesn't understand that we think it's wrong for them to cheat, [and that] the world thinks it's wrong for them to cheat. As long as we can continue that feeling among the team ... we're headed in the right direction. What happened to the older athletes, either through suspension or simply suspicion, has been a lesson to the young ones."

Ask yourself this...

■ How tempted would you be to take something that you knew was illegal, but you think could win you an Olympic gold medal?

■ How would your answer differ if you knew that all your competitors were taking that same substance?

■ Why ban performance drugs?

■ **Craig Masback supports drugs testing and bans for athletes that cheat.**

What do drugs have to do with me?

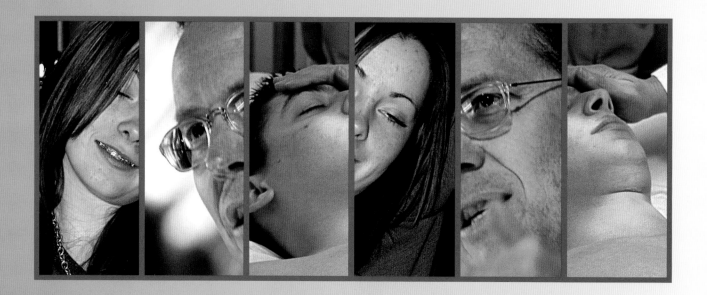

Probably everyone who reads this book will have deodorants and prescription drugs in their home. Many people have alcohol at home, and you may know someone who smokes cigarettes. You may even be aware of cannabis and crack cocaine use. But whether you have first hand experience of drugs, or have never thought about the subject before, consider whether you agree or disagree with the following statements on the right. Look at the responses to the questions and go back through the book. Use all this information to form your own opinions about drugs.

■ All drug addicts only have themselves to blame.

"I don't really think this is true. People have different reasons for becoming addicted to drugs. I think it has a lot to do with who you hang out with."
    (Anna, aged 10)

■ Anyone could become addicted to drugs.

"Yes, I agree. Look at how many people become addicted to smoking. Cigarettes are made to be addictive."
    (Leon, aged 9)

■ It's up to each person to decide what they do to their own bodies.

"Everyone has a choice. If an athlete is banned for taking enhancing drugs it's their own fault."
   (Jerome, aged 11)

■ If you don't want to take it – don't. It doesn't matter what your friends say.

"Who wrote this? What your friends say is the most important thing – who wants to be an outcast?"
   (Melinda, aged 12)

"Sometimes you have to stand up for yourself, and against your friends, so I agree with this."
   (Zoe, aged 11)

■ The more you know about drugs the more likely you are to experiment with them.

"I had to think about this one, and lots of people really disagree with me. I think it's true; if you didn't know anything about drugs, why would you take them?"
   (Jack, aged 9)

"I'm not so sure about this. Why would knowing more about smoking make you want to light up? If you know about the risks then you can make a proper decision."
   (Naseem, aged 10)

■ Government anti-drugs campaigns don't work.

"I think I need more information to answer this. How do I know they don't work?"
(Nimish, aged 11)

"Of course they don't work, otherwise no one would do drugs."
(Clinton, aged 10)

Websites

The websites below feature more information, news articles and stories that you can use to help form your own opinions. Use the information carefully and consider the source it comes from before drawing any conclusions.

www.talktofrank.com
UK government-backed website, featuring drugs information and an email connection for free drugs advice.

www.drugfree.org
This website from the Partnership for a Drug-Free America includes a section for teenagers, with moving personal accounts of drug addiction.

www.nida.nih.gov/ students.html
Website of the National Centre for Drug Abuse in the USA. This page contains lots of links to other drug education websites.

www.nzsda.co.nz
Home of the New Zealand Sports Drug Agency, helping to deter the use of drugs in sport and to promote educational programmes.

www.streetdrugs.org
Contains drugs information for pupils, teachers and parents, including facts, advice and a drugs index.

www.drugs.vibe.com.au/ drugs/index.asp
Australian government-backed website of "Deadly Vibes" magazine. It features stories and facts about drugs, plus a health and education section.

Glossary

Abuse – the wrong use of something.

Acupuncture – a physcial treatment where special needles are inserted into the skin. Some people believe it can help smokers to quit.

Addictive – when something contains a substance that encourages people to take more. For example, cigarettes are addictive because they contain the drug nicotine.

Alcohol poisoning – when the alcohol level in a person's blood is so high that some body functions stop working. It can also cause permanent damage to some internal organs.

Binge drinking – when someone drinks more than four alcoholic drinks in a row.

Counselling – when someone talks to a professional counsellor or therapist to help discuss and solve their problems.

Depression – a medical condition. A person suffering from depression feels deep unhappiness and low self-esteem for a long period of time.

High – the feeling produced by some drugs.

Hypocrite – someone who supports one viewpoint or belief but does something different through their actual behaviour.

Inhalation – breathing in a gas.

Junkie – another word for a drug addict.

Lung disease – there are many types of lung disease, including lung cancer, which is mainly caused by smoking.

Multiple sclerosis – a medical condition resulting in physical disorders, including speech impairment and paralysis.

Social services – part of the Department of Health that aims to help and support disadvantaged people.

Stillborn – when a baby is dead at birth.

Withdrawal symptoms – the condition experienced by a drug addict when they stop taking drugs. They can include anxiety, craving and uncontrollable shaking of the body.

www.dea.gov
Website of the US Drugs Enforcement Administration, featuring the latest drug trafficking, abuse and law enforcement news.

www.drugscope.org.uk
Website featuring D-World, a section with games, projects and drugs facts.

www.homeoffice.gov.uk/ drugs
Website outlining the UK government's fight against drugs, including statistics, strategies and links to other departments.

Index